One is Fun

Leona DeRosa Bodie

illustrated by
Catherine Baptista Davis

One is Fun

Leona DeRosa Bodie

illustrated by
Catherine Baptista Davis

One is Fun Second Edition
©2012 Leona DeRosa Bodie
©2012 Illustrations by Catherine Baptista Davis

All rights reserved. No part of this publication may be reproduced, stored in a retrieval system or transmitted in any form by any means electronic, mechanical, photocopying, recording or otherwise, except brief extracts for the purpose of reviews, without the permission of the publisher and copyright owner.

Published by
WRB Publishing
Palm City, FL 34990

wrb1174@att.net

**Logan is one.
He thinks one is fun.
One is fun.
Let's look at all he's done.**

**He talks in his crib
Before his parents wake,
Clapping his hands
To Patty Cake.**

**The sun is up, so Logan's up.
A boy's face framed in curls,
He sits and plays
On a blanket of blue swirls.**

**With a laugh and a giggle,
He reaches for the railing.
With a smile and a wiggle
On tiptoe, he's sailing.**

He smiles when Mommy
Carries him from his crib.
"Breakfast," she says,
But he won't wear a bib.

**Now that he has six tiny teeth,
Snacks are yummy.
He so loves when
Daddy tickles his tummy.**

**No, no, no! Not a baby,
He's a busy little boy.
Mommy and Daddy insist,
He's a perfect joy.**

First a crawl, then a wobble
But wait, he's walking!
Round the sofa, now a fine chase,
Logan's running and Daddy's gawking.

"See," Logan says,
Pointing to airplanes in the sky.
Mommy says, "Time for work."
So, he waves bye-bye.

**Grandpa watches Logan
In the town by the bay,
Every workday,
They laugh and play.**

Logan loves fresh air.
He giggles without a care,
Feeling breezes
In his curly golden hair.

**Only one, Logan loves
So many things.
He listens to music,
Dances and sings.**

Logan loves sharing
His books and toys
With other little
Girls and boys.

He likes when
Mommy holds him tight.
As soon as she sees him,
She laughs with delight.

**This little boy turns buttons,
Knobs and switches.
On lights, stereo and TV. Oh, oh!
Sometimes, there are glitches.**

It's a funny, sunny day,
No more to do inside.
Yea, Logan wants to play,
With all his friends outside.

**Everywhere Logan goes
Is fun for all, small or tall.
So his friends are sure to follow
Small or tall, they all play ball.**

Grandma's earrings jingle.
It's really a dilly.
Logan says, "Pretty."
So Aunt Nay-nay squeezes him silly.

Logan likes when Uncle James smiles at him, And lifts him Higher on a whim.

**Great Grandma loves holding
Logan on her lap.
Only a few minutes, before
He squirms, running for his cap.**

Sometimes they go to parks,
Or picnics, walks or rides
Or sometimes Logan goes
On swings and slides.

Sometimes they go to parks,
Or picnics, walks or rides
Or sometimes Logan goes
On swings and slides.

**Yellow letters on navy pants,
Spell Logan's a champ.
So says everyone,
Especially Gramp.**

**In the pool or the hot tub,
With warm water brimming
Grandpa takes
Logan swimming.**

When Daddy comes home, Logan runs to the door. He loves wrestling with Daddy on the floor.

Logan loves hearing
Uncle Paul play his guitar.
Logan strums on the strings
That's all he knows so far.

**Someday, all too soon,
Logan will ride a bicycle.
Today, his brown eyes sparkle,
As he rides his tricycle.**

Weekends by the sea,
Tan sand along the beach.
Logan sits building sandcastles,
While soaring seagulls screech.

**With Daddy's steady hand,
Logan can float!
Sometimes they even
Go out on the boat.**

**Scrub-a-dub dub in the tub,
Shampoo in his hair.
Logan loves
Suds and bubbles everywhere.**

**Soon Logan cuddles, cozy warm.
Time for bed, finally night
He rubs his eyes, and
Kisses goodnight.**

www.ingramcontent.com/pod-product-compliance
Lightning Source LLC
Chambersburg PA
CBHW041539040426
42446CB00002B/161